To Dejah M. Boykin,
Best Wishes!

O'Neil

Let's Explore Sea Turtles

Michael Patrick O'Neill
Batfish Books

O'Neill, Michael Patrick
Let's Explore Sea Turtles / Michael Patrick O'Neill
ISBN 978-0-9728653-2-6
LCCN 2005901568

Printed in China

Batfish Books
PO Box 32909
Palm Beach Gardens, FL 33420-2909
www.batfishbooks.com
Photographer's Website:
www.mpostock.com

10 9 8 7 6 5 4 3

Here come the ancient mariners.

Loggerhead Turtle

For over 100 Million Years, they've roamed the World's oceans.

Hawksbill Turtles

Other creatures have come and gone, and great changes have rocked our planet, but these prehistoric animals keep hanging on.

WHat MaKeS tHeM So toUgH?

Let's explore the mysterious lives of the peaceful hawksbill, the clever green, the giant leatherback and the mighty loggerhead and find out their secrets of survival.

HoW LoNg WiLL tHey LaSt?

Let's learn about the threats facing sea turtles and see how devoted people are helping them bounce back from the brink of extinction.

These turtles, named for their hawk-like beaks, live in the coastal waters of over 80 tropical countries and nest in the Caribbean, Indian Ocean and the South Pacific.

Hawksbill Turtle
The UnderWater Architect

With shells 3 ft. long and weighing about 150 lbs., hawksbills are on the small side when compared to other sea turtles.

But what they lack in size, they make up in friendliness. Easy-going, they allow divers to come close and check them out as they search the sea bottom for their favorite food – sponges.

In fact, these turtles eat so many sponges – each adult consumes up to 1,200 lbs. per year – they can change the look of the reef.

With the hawksbills trimming the sponges and keeping them short, corals then have a chance to grow.

For centuries, skilled craftsmen turned this species' attractive shell into items such as eyeglass frames, brush handles and jewelry.

Nowadays, many reefs are overgrown with sponges because there aren't enough of these "underwater landscapers" around.

Green Turtle
The Crafty Vegetarian

Sea grass and algae make up most of this turtle's diet.

Growing to 5 ft. in length and 450 lbs., the green is a jumbo-sized, clever turtle with many tricks that help it thrive in the deep.

For example, to escape sharks, this smart animal will often crawl up on a deserted beach to avoid the dangerous predators.

During cold winters, they may even hibernate in the muddy bottom of a lagoon. Asleep and buried in the muck, these sleepyheads absorb oxygen through the skin and don't have to surface to breathe.

This marine reptile gets its name from the green-colored fat and muscle inside its body.

THIS SPECIES IS ANOTHER EXAMPLE OF HOW SEA TURTLES ARE CITIZENS OF THE WORLD.

GREENS ARE FOUND IN NEARLY 140 COUNTRIES.

It will take at least 25 years for this hatchling to mature. Since they grow so slowly and breed so late in life, we must do everything possible – globally – to protect them. Otherwise, they don't have a fighting chance.

The Leatherback

This colossus ranks as one of the animal kingdom's most incredible marvels.

This turtle is named after its soft leathery shell.

The fastest growing reptile in the world and one of the largest, the leatherback can reach 11 ft. in length and 2,000 lbs. in weight.

To think this giant gets as heavy as a saltwater crocodile by eating jellyfish – a food that's mostly water – is astounding.

The major nesting sites for this nomadic species are Trinidad, Suriname and Guyana in South America and Gabon in West Africa. Smaller populations nest in the Caribbean, South Africa and New Guinea.

Massive, oar-like flippers will take this leatherback hatchling on voyages of epic proportions. Crisscrossing the planet is part of daily life for leatherbacks. And they do it in comfort: A thick coat of insulating fat and huge body mass keep them warm even when they visit frigid places like Alaska, Greenland and New Zealand.

Did you know this species belongs to an elite team of deep-sea divers?

Researchers followed a leatherback plunging to an amazing 4,000 ft.! Other sea turtles grow hard, rigid shells, but leatherbacks' flex and compress as they descend to those incredible depths.

Loggerhead Turtle
The Toughest of the Bunch

A male loggerhead patrols a South Florida reef.

Loggerheads grow to 4 ft. and tip the scales at over 400 lbs., and although they are not as large as greens and leatherbacks, they're the hardiest. Simply put, these turtles are built like army tanks!

The head, encased in a tough helmet of bone and skin, matches a basketball in size and gives the turtle its name. Thick leather skin and a rugged shell protect them from all but the largest sharks.

Their main weapon for fighting and feeding is a vise-like jaw that easily tears apart conch, crabs, fish and other unlucky prey.

While loggerheads can be found worldwide, Florida has the largest number of nesting females anywhere, over 19,000. Oman, Greece and Australia also have important populations.

Loggerhead hatchlings have the courage of a lion and the heart of a champion.

From the moment they leave the nest, they're fighting desperate odds, as only one in 1,000 will make it.

Raccoons, foxes, birds and crabs eat many babies – and that's just on the beach. When they enter the surf, a new gang of hunters lies in wait.

Although they seem doomed from the very beginning, the hatchlings are fearless and nearly unstoppable.

Driven by a force we still don't fully understand, they leave on a journey that lasts many years and takes them to the most distant corners of the sea.

Will this little champ make it?

Young turtles swim for days until they find a patch of sargassum. This floating seaweed is like a grocery store at sea. There, they find plenty to eat – bugs, tiny crabs, plants and even oil droplets!

DeStiNatioN: UNKNoWN

In the past, no one knew where Florida loggerheads went after leaving the beaches as hatchlings. Scientists called this phase in the turtles' lives the "lost years." Eventually, they learned the babies rode the Gulf Stream and ended up in the North Atlantic near Europe. After some 10 years adrift, they returned home.

You would have a hard time recognizing our little champ as an adult. The one-time featherweight is now a heavyweight contender.

A Ray of Hope

All over the world, people work hard to save sea turtles, and a big chunk of this effort takes place in conservation centers close to where sea turtles live.

Scientists, vets and volunteers come together on a daily basis to protect nesting areas, treat injured turtles, study them and educate the public.

Everyone rolls up their sleeves to make a difference and show what's possible when we all work together.

Let's drop by and see what's going on in one of these special places.

The Marinelife Center

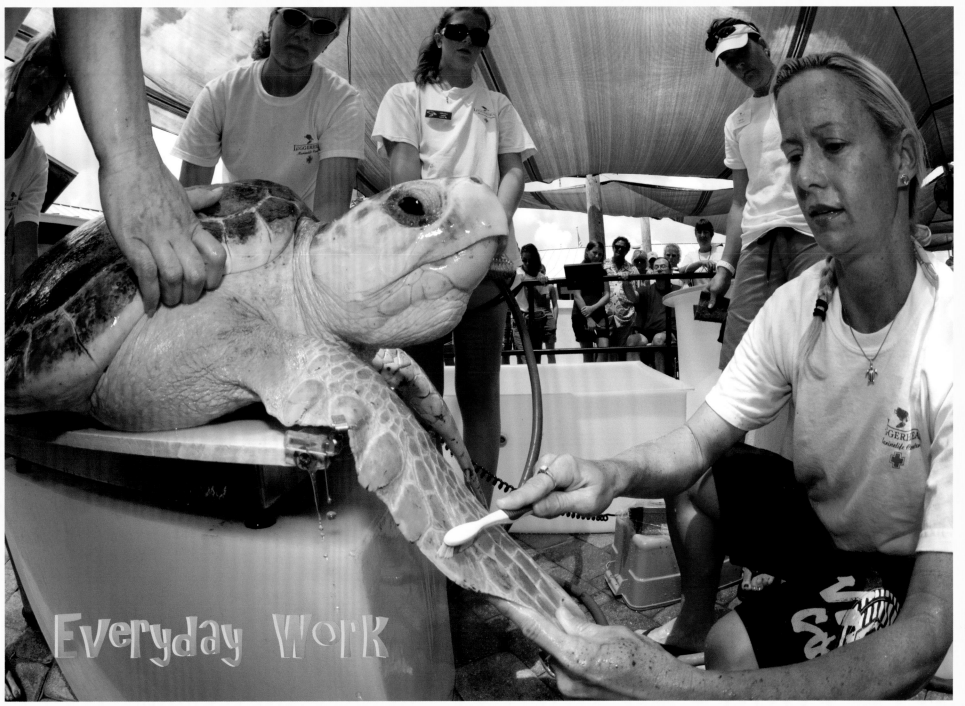

Everyday Work

Volunteers clean a loggerhead.

Something Special is about to take place...

Matilda's Big Day

Matilda, an enormous loggerhead, is ready to go back to the ocean after recuperating from a cold.

This gorgeous old girl knows her caretakers are up to something.

One! Two! Three! LIFT!!!

At nearly 300 lbs., she is more than a handful.

HomeWard bound

Matilda swims into the surf as the crowd watches.

A volunteer comforts her on the way to the beach.

Free
at Last!

Hawksbill Turtle

Their Future is in our Hands.

Hundreds of years ago, there were more sea turtles than stars in the night sky. Unfortunately, those days are long gone.

These deep divers, marathon swimmers, underwater architects and master navigators can do it all, but can they survive us?

The answer to this question depends on how committed we are to saving them. Is it worth the effort? Let's see:

1. Sea turtle tourism generates money and jobs for rich and poor countries alike.

2. Sea turtles are keystone species that reflect the overall health of the oceans.

3. By keeping reefs healthy, they help us out, too. People worldwide depend on these marine habitats for food and medicines.

4. The contribution of sea turtles to the planet's biodiversity and beauty is incalculable.

Well, is it worth the effort? What do you think?

Green Turtle